The BRILLIANT
Church

Rediscovering
God's Kingdom Church Model

DR. MARTIN WILLIAMS

DR. MARTIN WILLIAMS

MARTIN WILLIAMS INTERNATIONAL ©

ISBN-13: 978-0996096225

DR. MARTIN WILLIAMS

Disclaimer

For questions or comments regarding any aspect of this book, visit www.martinwilliams.org

DR. MARTIN WILLIAMS

DEDICATION

I would like to dedicate this book...

To my faithful and supportive wife, Lynnell, I sincerely thank you for your undying love and acceptance of me, my vision and my assignment. Also for being my first and most distinguished church member. Thank you for getting this manuscript out of my head and onto these pages. Let's keep it going!

To my children, Callie and Joshua, who are so far ahead of me at their young age. I remain grounded to my allegiance and vow to God and our family because your faces are always before me. My commitment and love for you both and your mother cannot be measured.

To Drs. Myles and Ruth Munroe of Bahamas Faith Ministry in Nassau, Bahamas, who taught me all I know about the King and His kingdom. I am forever grateful for the incredible spiritual parents you will always be in my Kingdom pursuit, marriage, parenting, businesses, and my life. It will always be my desire and intent to honor you both for the rest of my days on earth.

To Bishop Robert Strong of Kossuth Church of God in Christ in St. Louis, Missouri for your constant mentorship, wisdom, discipleship and love. You have always been there for me.

To the board of directors, presbytery, leaders and covenant partners of Ambassadors Worship Center; there's absolutely no Kingdom Church like what our culture has built! Thank you for your unwavering commitment, serving and embracing the vision of our house in order that the Kingdom not just be heard but also seen! I could not have achieved the measure of success to date without your love, faithfulness and submission to my gift as your shepherd.

ACKNOWLEDGMENTS

Completing this book has taken over 20 years of learning, studying, observation and even experimentation. But most importantly, I must credit all the wisdom I have gained and learned from numerous great people. However, it's the people, who have dedicated their lives to my assignment that are the real difference makers. The awareness of other people's contribution in this process never escapes me.

I am the sum total, of the efforts and involvement of my parents, my sister, Mattie Pearl Williams; who raised us after our parents died, my family, mentors and coaches that have entered and exited my life. However, it is without a doubt that the people of Ambassadors Worship Center in Omaha, Nebraska that have impacted me the most as it relates to this particular project.

Simply put, I would not have had a reason to endure the hardship that I faced in developing the ideas and models of Kingdom churches. The motivation came from spending time with you and praying for the courage to launch the concept of what I believe defines a Kingdom church model.

Your earnest desire to know the King in a real way encouraged and challenged me to strive for God's original idea. It is difficult to describe my thankfulness to the people of this church. The honest truth is the AWC Nation, as I call it, has had a big part of making the Martin Luther Williams that I am.

Lastly, this book would not have been developed and now completed without my excellent team of administrators. I sincerely thank and appreciate my wife, Lynnell, Leslie McAuley, Rebecca Crawford and Stacey Flowers for joining my struggle in seeing this project as worthy of their time and incredible administrative skills.

Most importantly, words fail to express how grateful I am once again to my very dedicated and talented executive staff for always being willing and available to seeing my project completed.

TABLE OF CONTENTS

Preface: The Church i

Introduction i

Chapter 1 1
Back to the Beginning

Chapter 2 11
The Gate of Heaven

Chapter 3 19
Wherever the Waters Go

Chapter 4 37
Ignorant Gatekeepers

Chapter 5 49
The Unconscious Church

Chapter 6 59
The World is the Lord's

Chapter 7 69
No, I'll Use My Church

Chapter 8 83
What is the Church?

Chapter 9 97
Brilliance: What Does it Mean?

Chapter 10 113
You and the Church

The Church

"Church" is a religious word. It is inherently religious in meaning. We speak of going to church, of building a church, of going into the church, of running the church, of starting a church, of the authority of the church, of the organization of the church, and the list could go on. The point is that we really use the word as it is defined in our Western dictionary but not in context with God's ideal of Church. The Church... It stretches far beyond what you see. It accomplishes more than we dreamed was possible.

Not every culture is individualistic. But in the Western world, we tend to look up to Lone Rangers.

Our heroes are strong and self-sufficient, and they tend

to walk alone. Very often, the Western church tends toward this type of individualism. We hear Jesus's call to take up our cross and follow Him, and we decide to follow no matter what anyone else says or does. Of course, this is the right response, but we need to be careful here. While every individual needs to obey Jesus's call to follow, we cannot follow Jesus as individuals.

The proper context for every disciple maker is the Church. It is impossible to make disciples aside from the Church of Jesus Christ. Look at it from this perspective: the New Testament is full of commands to do this or that for "one another." Love one another, pray for one another, encourage one another, etc. So how can we teach people to "observe all that I have commanded" if they have no one to love, pray for, or encourage? It's impossible to "one another" yourself. It's impossible to follow Jesus alone. We can't claim to follow Jesus if we neglect the Church He created, the Church He died for, the Church He entrusted His mission to.

First, let's make sure that we are not guilty of belittling God's Church in any way. It's not a social club; it's not a building, and it's not an option.

The Church is life and death. The Church is God's strategy for reaching our world. What we do inside the

Church matters. We tend to equate church life with events and programs. But these are not what make a church. Programs are helpful to the extent that they facilitate the life and mission of the Church, but we can't equate well-attended events with the health of the Church.

God cares about the way we love each other and the way we pursue His mission. The Church is a group of redeemed people that live and serve together in such a way that their lives and communities are transformed.

What matters is your interaction with the people God has placed in your life. If you are not connected with other Christians, serving and being served, challenging and being challenged, then you are not living as He desires, and the Church is not functioning as He intended.

Throughout the Bible, we see pictures of the global church (which includes all followers of Jesus in all locations) and the local church (which includes particular followers of Jesus in a particular location). Out of 114 times that the "Church" is mentioned in the New Testament, at least ninety of them refer to specific local gatherings of believers who have banded together for fellowship and a mission. God intends for every follower of Jesus to be a part of such a gathering under the servant leadership of pastors, who shepherd the Church for the glory of God.

Despite the clear priority that the Bible places on believers being part of a local church, many followers of Christ try to live the Christian life apart from serious, personal commitment to a local church.

The reasons are many. We are self-reliant and self-sufficient, and the kind of mutual interdependence and even submission and accountability to others that the Bible talks about frightens us. We are often indecisive, hopping from one church to another looking for the "perfect place" and the "perfect people." Many of us have been hurt in the past by things that have happened to or around us in the Church, and others of us simply don't see the importance of being specifically connected to a local church.

But the Bible says the local church is important. God has entrusted local churches with godly leaders who teach us His Word and care for our souls. God has united us together in local churches to keep one another from sinning and straying from Christ. God has commanded us to gather together in local assemblies where we preach God's Word, celebrate the Lord's Supper, baptize new believers, and pray for and encourage one another (Acts 2:42; Hebrews 10:24–25). Then we scatter to care for believers and to share the gospel of the Kingdom with unbelievers (Acts

2:43–47).

Clearly, being a disciple and making disciples involves committing your life to a local church where you are joined together with other believers under biblical leadership to grow in the likeness of Christ and to express the love of Christ to the world around you.

INTRODUCTION

[13] When Jesus came into the region of Caesarea Philippi, He asked His disciples, saying, "Who do men say that I, the Son of Man, am?"

[14] So they said, "Some *say* John the Baptist, some Elijah, and others Jeremiah or one of the prophets."

[15] He said to them, "But who do you say that I am?"

[16] Simon Peter answered and said, "You are the Christ, the Son of the living God."

[17] Jesus answered and said to him, "Blessed are you, Simon Bar-Jonah, for flesh and blood has not revealed *this* to you, but My Father who is in heaven. [18] And I also say to you that you are Peter, **and on this rock I will build My church**, and the gates of Hades shall not prevail against it.

Matthew 16: 13-18 (NKJV)

The Carpenter

It seemed just like a normal day. All of his materials look the same. Carpentry tools look the same. He had been carving wood all his life. It was a trade that he learned from his father. He had become very excellent at this skill. As he picked up his carving tools to begin his work it was almost like the wood was calling and challenging him to do something he had never done. As he tried to ignore the thoughts in his head, the inner voice became stronger and stronger.

His tools seem to cut through the wood like butter as if they had been sharpened to perfection. The more and more he carved the more peace he found. If he wasn't stretching his imagination, he would have thought that the wood and his carving tools had met before. They acted as though they were one. Obviously you don't finish a masterpiece in one day. So he worked on this block of wood for weeks. One hour after the other, and one day after several weeks, the wood began to finally take shape.

After working faithfully on the carving, he started to feel something special, as if this piece of wood would be very important to someone. As if it would affect and change someone's life. At last it dawned on him this could be the most important piece he had actually ever carved.

Have you ever felt that way? For instance, as if you're embarking on something significant all alone. That is exactly the way I feel as I start to construct this book. The information that I'll share in this book has changed my life. It has changed my view of the world. It has changed my view of God. It has changed my view of myself. More importantly it has changed my view of what I believed about the Church.

Because of how this information has changed my life I want to make sure that I share it with the world. I'm motivated to communicate the secrets of the Kingdom in a way that it affects how the Church operates. I am determined to redefine the original idea of what I believe God's view of the Church is to be in the earth.

It is a simple fact that we live in desperate times. The world is changing around us at an astounding pace. Social systems are failing. It is becoming very difficult to find peace on earth. The significance of the Church is waning in society. It will even seem that the Church could become irrelevant, and more dangerously, the fact remains that we do not have godly leaders in position to help navigate through this pool of chaos.

In preparing this manuscript, I hope to enlighten you on how significant and very important the role of the Church is in recovering God's original idea. You will understand that **the Church will play a major role in re-capturing peace on earth and ultimately fulfilling God's primary will for mankind.**

I do have a request of you. I ask that you open your mind to **"think"**, to consider, to question, to listen and then draw conclusions from what you learn.

DR. MARTIN WILLIAMS

CHAPTER
1

DR. MARTIN WILLIAMS

Back to the Beginning

We think that everything begins and ends with us.
~Dr. Myles Munroe

Genesis 2:8-14 The Lord God planted a garden eastward in Eden, and there He put the man whom He had formed. 9 And out of the ground the Lord God made every tree grow that is pleasant to the sight and good for food. The tree of life was also in the midst of the garden, and the tree of the knowledge of good and evil. 10 Now a river went out of Eden to water the garden, and from there it parted and became four riverheads. 11 The name of the first is Pishon; it is the one which skirts the whole land of Havilah, where there is gold. 12 And the gold of that land is good. Bdellium and the onyx stone are there. 13 The name of the second river is Gihon; it is the one which goes around the whole land of Cush. 14 The name of the third river is Hiddekel; it is the one which goes toward the east of Assyria. The fourth river is the Euphrates.

The Original Plan

If you want to know the heart of God it will be important to use the Law of First Mention. The Law of First Mention is simply what it says. It means to find the first place in the Bible where God mentions a concept or precept. You will find that this Law of First Mention is usually the purest form of God's mind. In other words, God simply states His original intent to mankind.

Why is the mind of God so important? For us as kingdom citizens the heart of God is the most important thing to us. If we don't have the heart of God we will never realize the fulfillment of His desire. This section of Scripture shows us the original heart of God; it tells us how God thinks!

What if the life we're living right now wasn't the original plan of God? What if the plan of God has been lost in our religious practices? What if your religious denominational practices violate God's intent? Perhaps we've been teaching and doing good things but not teaching and doing the *right* things according to God's heart. It is time we really take a closer look.

In the original state of Adam's life, Adam was placed in a garden called Eden. Dr. Myles Munroe[i] taught us that Eden literally means the spot for the moment where the

4

presence of the Lord is an open door to heaven. What does this mean? This means that wherever Adam was, there was not any distance nor any difference between him and heaven. Wherever Adam was he had a direct line of communication to God. From there he could communicate with God and rule the earth at the same time. This is literally heaven on earth!

Because of the purpose of this book I want to emphasize Genesis 2:10–15. It is clear that from Adam's living space and headquarters (Eden) that a river went out from him and turned into four outflows. I have heard many sermons/lessons about this verse and the most common interpretation is that you need to have four streams of income.

But if you reread this, Adam did not have four streams of income. He had four streams of outflow. Most people talk about having four streams of income, but in our Kingdom, you only have one flow of income that is from the Lord. You become the outflow. From your space and from your life, you water the earth as God's representative.

For lots of you reading this book this may be the first time you've heard of this concept, but it is God's original plan for mankind.

Genesis 2:10 15 A river watering the garden flowed from Eden; from there it was separated into four headwaters. 11 The name of the first is the Pishon; it winds through the entire land of Havilah, where there is gold. 12 (The gold of that land is good; aromatic resin[d] and onyx are also there.) 13 The name of the second river is the Gihon; it winds through the entire land of Cush.[e] 14 The name of the third river is the Tigris; it runs along the east side of Ashur. And the fourth river is the Euphrates. 15 The Lord God took the man and put him in the Garden of Eden to work it and take care of it.

These four rivers had plenty of prosperity in them, from gold to precious stone and resin. All of the bounty of the earth was in the rivers from Adam's environment. Adam was in charge of watering, nourishing and managing the entire earth from Eden. This is the place where heaven kissed earth.

It's obvious what God gave Adam. God gave him dominion, authority, rulership, management and the responsibility to dominate the earth. Adam was given a power and position in God's kingdom on the earth. So all of these things he lost or we can say he simply abdicated his role and duties when he decided to disobey God.

What Did We Lose?

We are all familiar with the phrase "fallen." But what

does it really mean to fall? What did he fall from? Exactly what did Adam lose? To get the answer to these questions maybe we should ask "what did he originally have?" What did God give him?

> *Genesis 3:22-24 Then the Lord God said, "Behold, the man has become like one of Us, to know good and evil. And now, lest he put out his hand and take also of the Tree of Life, and eat, and live forever" -- 23 therefore the Lord God sent him out of the garden of Eden to till the ground from which he was taken. 24 So He drove out the man; and He placed cherubim at the east of the garden of Eden, and a flaming sword which turned every way, to guard the way to the Tree of Life.*

One of the most important things that Adam lost was the environment from which to rule. He lost Eden! He lost the open door to heaven. He lost that spot where there was no distance or difference between him and heaven. He lost his

Adam did not lose Heaven!

direct link to God's realm. He lost the opportunity to manage the earth with heaven's wisdom. Adam did not lose Heaven! He lost both his sonship and rulership to have dominion on earth.

In my thinking it is easy to underestimate this loss. After all, this is why earth was created. It was created as an additional territory that God could rule without being here.

7

God would rule this new territory by putting His Spirit inside man. Man was stamp proxy of God on planet earth. There would be eternal rule on earth as long as man could be in constant communication with God. And from man's environment God could bless the entire planet. Eden, the place where man once lived, would be the entrance to everything good and acceptable according to God's will.

Because of Adam's disobedience, he was commanded to leave. As a matter of fact, he was escorted out by the angels. To make it worse, God assigned an angel to guard the entrance to keep him from coming back into the garden.

What if God had allowed Adam to stay in Eden after eating from the Tree of the Knowledge of Good and Evil? God's concern was noted in verse 22, "lest he put out his hand and take also of the Tree of Life, and eat, and live forever". God knew that if Adam ate from the Tree of Life in that current condition, he would be like that forever.

When Adam fell, he lost direct connection with God. He was no longer qualified to be God's onsite representative. If he stayed like that forever, he would never be redeemable. He would never be an outflow. Even though Adam disobeyed, God knew that if he left the garden, he could eventually be returned to his rightful position. God was so concerned about protecting Eden from a fallen man and protecting a fallen man from Eden that He was willing to sever the direct link to heaven.

So is God protecting Adam from Eden or is God protecting Eden from Adam? Either way, the result is the same. Adam lost the spot! This was the most important place on earth.

DR. MARTIN WILLIAMS

CHAPTER
2

DR. MARTIN WILLIAMS

The Gate of Heaven

The Bible is not to be tampered with!
~Dr. Martin Williams

It is emotionally disturbing to talk about a time when heaven kissed earth. Disturbing because in Genesis 3 Adam lost his place called Eden. Despite what he had, an instant and complete connection to heaven was lost because of his sin. So, the rest of the Bible, is God's process of returning us back to Genesis 1 and 2. Simply put, it is God's strategy to get us to reconnect back to His original plan.

Let's read the account of Jacob's rediscovery of the heart of God.

Genesis 28:10-17 Now Jacob went out from Beersheba and went toward Haran. 11 So he came to a certain place and stayed there all night, because the sun had set. And he took one of the stones of that place and put it at his head, and he lay down in that place to sleep. 12 Then he dreamed, and behold, a ladder was set up on the earth, and its top reached to heaven; and there the angels of God were ascending and descending on it. 13 And behold, the Lord stood above it and said: "I am the Lord God of Abraham your father and the God of Isaac; the land on which you lie I will give to you and your descendants. 14 Also your descendants shall be as the dust of the earth; you shall spread abroad to the west and the east, to the north and the south; and in you and in your seed all the families of the earth shall be blessed. 15 Behold, I am with you and will keep you wherever you go, and will bring you back to this land; for I will not leave you until I have done what I have spoken to you." 16 Then Jacob awoke from his sleep and said, "Surely the Lord is in this place, and I did not know it." 17 And he was afraid and said, "How awesome is this place! This is none other than the house of God, and this is the gate of heaven!"

Many of you can remember that this is the account of Jacob running from his brother Esau after he had stolen his birthright. As a matter of fact, history accounts that his father and his brother, Esau, had made a vow to chase him down and kill him. Jacob was on the run simply trying to get away from his brother. Isn't it amazing how sometimes we are trying to run away from God and we end up running smack dab into Him?

When you are traveling through the wilderness, it is important not to travel at night. It is easy to lose your way and there are wild beasts that hunt at night. Jacob decided to take a rest. While he was sleeping he had a dream. His dream is really interesting; ever since I was a little boy I've heard people talk about Jacob's ladder. But what does it really mean? Was it really a ladder as we know it? Let's explore.

He sees a ladder, and the base of this ladder is on the earth. The top of the ladder is extended into heaven. At the top of this ladder stands the Lord. Angels are ascending and then descending on this ladder, going up and down continually carrying answers back and forth to God's people.

This is a direct depiction of Genesis 2. This is the restoration of the heaven and the earth coming together as one, the place where there is neither difference nor any distance between heaven and earth. This is the same space where angels ascend taking the prayers of the people of God, and they descend bringing answers from heaven. This ladder is a place of power and dominion because it has a direct link to heaven. It is simply the place where God's will and His intent can be given to man in order to operate on earth.

From the top of the ladder in Jacob's dream, the Lord reminds him of this promise to his grandfather Abraham. This promise Jacob has heard all of his life from his father, Isaac. The Lord would give them the earth to reign and they would outnumber the sand and the stars. The re-account of the promise of God does not surprise Jacob because for generations these words had been spoken.

However, two things did surprise Jacob. He was surprised that the voice of the Lord reminded him that He would keep him safe and bring him back to this spot on the earth. Secondly, he was surprised that the Lord was in that place. Just imagine being out in a desert of rocks, sand and extreme heat; it's more like the wilderness. But God had chosen this place to meet with Jacob. Haven't you been puzzled by where God has met you?

The most important part of this story is what Jacob says to God. Jacob has a revelation that we all should take note of because this revelation points back to the original intent of God.

> Genesis 28:17 And he was afraid and said, "How awesome is this place! This is none other than the house of God, and this is the gate of heaven!"

In the passage, the word I bring to your attention is

"afraid". Jacob had never had this feeling before; he had never had this experience with God before. This was his first time managing this feeling. Can you imagine lying down to rest for the night and having an awesome dream like this? So, upon waking up he was afraid like the times you can recall in some of your disturbing dreams.

Next, he was awestruck at the place he was in. This was the ultimate place. This was the place like no other place on earth, the place where heaven met earth, the place of the ladder. I remind you he did not say God is awesome, he said this place is awesome. What place was he talking about? What was the significance of Jacob's words?

He calls it the House of God, the place of God's presence. The House of God can be translated simply into the Church. In Jacob's eyes the Church was awesome.

And lastly his phrase, "this is the Gate of Heaven." It doesn't matter how many times I read the Scripture, I'm still amazed that the heart of God is for the Church to be known as the Gate of Heaven.

What is a gate you ask? A gate is a place of entrance and it is a place of exit. It is the place where things come in and a place where things go out. It is the place of legal entrance. Gates are the only authorized entrance point. It is the place that's guarded and watched. Gates are important to every city because it's a normal passage.

During Jacob's time, the only way a city could protect itself was to build a wall around the entire city, so a gate in the wall was the only legal entrance and exit into the city. The city officials appointed specific people to sit at the gate and judge what could come in and what could go out. They were protecting the people in the city by deciding what was allowed and what was not allowed. If something didn't come in through the gate, it was considered illegal!

—

The Church is the place of entrance for the heart of God.

Now let's look again at Jacob's revelation: anything that God has decided that He wants to do on the earth, He has chosen the Church to be the gate to bring it through. The Church is the place of entrance for the heart of God. God wants to use the Church as the originator, the innovator, and the initiator of executing His will.

CHAPTER
3

DR. MARTIN WILLIAMS

Wherever the Waters Go

The Kingdom of God is advancing.
~Dr. Martin Williams

In God's eyes, He never considered that the Church would become irrelevant. I'm sure He never wanted humans on earth to look to politicians, governments, nonprofits and the United Nations to answer their problems. I'm certain that He never expected inventions and innovations or answers to issues to come from outside the Church. After all, He created the Church to share His mind with mankind on earth.

Here is another biblical example:

Ezekiel 47:1-12 Then he brought me back to the door of the temple; and there was water, flowing from under the threshold of the temple toward the east, for the front of the temple faced east; the water was flowing from under the right side of the temple, south of the altar. 2 He brought me out by way of the north gate, and led me around on the outside to the outer gateway that faces east; and there was water, running out on the right side. 3 And when the man went out to the east with the line in his hand, he measured one thousand cubits, and he brought me through the waters; the water came up to my ankles. 4 Again he measured one thousand and brought me through the waters; the water came up to my knees. Again he measured one thousand and brought me through; the water came up to my waist. 5 Again he measured one thousand, and it was a river that I could not cross; for the water was too deep, water in which one must swim, a river that could not be crossed. 6 He said to me, "Son of man, have you seen this?" Then he brought me and returned me to the bank of the river. 7 When I returned, there, along the bank of the river, were very many trees on one side and the other. 8 Then he said to me: "This water flows toward the eastern region, goes down into the valley, and enters the sea. When it reaches the sea, its waters are healed. 9 And it shall be that every living thing that moves, wherever the rivers go, will live. There will be a very great multitude of fish, because these waters go there; for they will be healed, and everything will live wherever the river goes. 10 It shall be that fishermen will stand by it from En Gedi to En Eglaim; they will be places for spreading their nets. Their fish will be of the same kinds as the fish of the Great Sea, exceedingly many. 11 But its swamps and marshes will not be healed; they will be given over to salt. 12 Along the bank of the river, on this side and that, will grow all kinds of trees used for food; their leaves will not wither, and their fruit will not fail. They will bear fruit every month, because their water flows from the sanctuary. Their fruit will be for food, and their leaves for medicine."

Just for background, it is important for us to know that Ezekiel is writing from Babylon. He was part of the initial group that was taken captive by King Nebuchadnezzar while King Jehoichin was king over Judah. When Ezekiel was taken with the second group of slaves from Israel – God command him to write! His job was to write to the captives in Babylon and remind them of the will of God for them and the temple. Often God would give him dreams and visions because nothing that was around him looked like the original plan God had for them. What is God saying to you through dreams and visions? Has He commanded you to write?

In Ezekiel's dream, God showed Ezekiel something extraordinary but historical. He shows him a temple, a place of worship, the House of God with water flowing from underneath it. The water was flowing from underneath the threshold of the temple flowing to the east. Again we see from Adam's space a river is flowing from the original point called the House of God but flowing out to the world.

Interestingly, it was just like the river that left Eden where Adam lived. It got deeper and wider and more influential after he left the temple. It was deep enough for his ankles at first, then his knees, his waist, and then deep enough to swim in. This is what God expects from the Church that revelation knowledge and innovation would increase as the people of God walk out the plan of God from the House of God.

In the dream, Ezekiel is told that no matter where this river goes there will be trees on each side of it, and everything living in the river will be safe and healthy. With spectacular confidence he is told that when this river reaches the bitter seeds it will even heal disease. One river can heal the seeds of bitterness. Those are powerful waters.

Just for a moment I want to remind you of how important the Church should be in your life. No matter where you go, no matter where you live, you want to be a part of a life-giving church. The Church is the only hope for the earth and for mankind ever getting back on track. If we can get the Church in order, the waters from the Church will bring healing to our society and healing to our world. If you are a functioning part of a local church, God

The Church is the only hope for the earth and for mankind ever getting back on track.

will give meaning to your life and position you to bring answers to a world that is in dire need of answers and Kingdom leadership. Again, the Church is the most important entity on planet earth!

The last thing Ezekiel is told is that on each side of the river there will be a multitude of trees, many trees of all types. These trees were special. First, they would be along the bank where the river flows. Secondly, their leaves would never fail and they would bear fruit all year long. The fruit and the leaves could be used for food and for healing medicine and all of this would happen because the water flowed from the temple. A river came out of the House of God.

I know you're excited to read the Scriptures also. I have an expectation in my heart that God is about to do something miraculous with His Church worldwide. We are going to grow trees inside our churches.

Trees are a symbol of culture. They grow deep into the ground, tap into water sources and wrap their roots around rocks. They produce shelter, food and healing medicine for the community. They are like tall, strong people who come together to build members of churches. They stand together along the bank of the river flowing out of church and become powerful, influential and bring healing to the world. These are exciting days to really know and be able to articulate your church's culture.

Creating your church's culture doesn't happen by accident. The truth is, I could walk into your church today and ask, "Why do you do that?" (that being a program,

Culture is completely misunderstood without a vision!

tradition, practice, use of terminology, etc.) and you would probably have any number of reasons for your, or your church's behavior. And probably buried somewhere among your answers would be, "That's just the way we do things around here." Therein lies the simplest definition of culture - **the way we do things around here.**

Unfortunately, few churches create their culture on purpose. Instead, they drift into a culture. But it doesn't have to be that way. Culture is completely misunderstood without a vision!

What Is A Church Culture?

So what is a culture? Culture is the sum of attitudes, customs and beliefs that distinguishes one group of people from another. Culture is transmitted through language, food, music, arts and rituals passed down through generations. Culture also refers to the cumulative deposit of knowledge, experiences, beliefs, values, religion and communication.

A church's culture is very important! It can be defined as an organization's culture as its "artifacts, espoused beliefs and values, and basic underlying assumptions." A culture is the make-up of a church's DNA which includes a church's behavior, values, and beliefs.

A church's **behavior** includes "all that you would see, hear, and feel as you first encounter the congregation." Worship style, the nature of the sermon, the ways in which members interact with each other, church signage, etc., are all behavioral artifacts of the church's culture. If church culture were an apple, behavior would be the peel. It is easily observable and forms the outer layer of the culture.

A church's **values** are the beliefs that the church actually lives out. If the church believes evangelism is important, it only becomes a value when church members actually evangelize. Values denote what the church cares about the most. It is the single most important attribute of making a culture unique and set apart from other cultures.

A church's **beliefs** are its convictions or opinions that a person holds to be true about the church and its world as based on limited proof." Significantly, the church may not always act on its beliefs (when beliefs are acted upon they become values), but they all have beliefs. Beliefs form the deepest layer of culture. The church's beliefs are the core of the cultural apple. Any organizational change in values and behaviors must occur at the level of a church's beliefs or assumptions, which is the most difficult level to change. Analyzing things such as the church's leadership, values, vision statement, structure, worship services, and the

"Culture eats strategy for breakfast."

activities of members during the week can reveal a church's culture. Culture is important because it shapes everything about the way things are done in the church. Strategies easily come and go, but culture is deeply imbedded and difficult to change. Peter Drucker, a pioneer in management research, once said, "Culture eats strategy for breakfast." A key to effective church leadership is to understand a church's culture as it is presently and shaping it in Biblical ways for the future. If you can shape the culture of your church, you can change the trajectory and total life of the church. The following are three practical ways to shape the culture of your church:

The Power of the Word of God

Effective leaders will shape their church's culture in ways that reflect obedience to the Word of God. Scripture is "profitable" to equip believers "for every good work" (2 Timothy 3:16). The most powerful way to shape and change a church's culture is through teaching what God's Word has to say about the Church. When Jesus wanted to change the culture of the temple in Jerusalem (the way things were done behaviorally), He did so by confronting them with God's Word (Mark 11:15-19). "It is written..." is the most effective way of addressing change.

Many people will not change what they believe simply because the pastor believes it. They need to be shown from the Bible why such-and-such proposal is being made, or why a particular objective in the church is — being pursued. Also some folks believe *The Word of* they know more Word than their pastor *God will* *always be the* which causes a world of other problems *final* within the culture. God speaks to the *authority!* pastor and it should be peaceful confirmation inside the congregation. The Word of God will always be the final authority!

The Power of Leadership

Everything rises and falls on leadership. Research has shown leaders provide more influence in shaping a church's culture than any other organizational factor. Leaders shape culture in a number of ways.

First, leaders set direction and cast vision. The focus of church members on the future of the church is vital. If the vision is focused inwardly, it will not take long before the culture of the church is selfish and inwardly focused. If the vision statement calls for great sacrifice in reaching the nations, the culture will begin to reflect an expectation of sacrifice in all things.

Second, leaders shape culture through the use of language and terminology. Whether it is in the pulpit, in the vision statement, on church signage, etc., language impacts the way people behave, what they value, and ultimately what they begin to assume and believe. Often, the church will begin to use the language the pastor uses. If you can get the key leaders of the church to speak the same language and emphasize the same terms, the church members will soon learn to care and think about those ideas. After a few years, the church reflects the leadership. Be intentional about the things you emphasize. Remember, even the young ones must embrace the culture.

—

Remember, even the young ones must embrace the culture.

Third, the way the pastor responds in critical moments in the life of the church shapes culture. For instance, when a pastor responds to a crisis with a calm confidence in God's sovereignty, the people will learn from that. These are great moments to disciple the people and shape the culture of the church. During these awkward times of trials is one of the best opportunities to provoke the congregation in their faith.

Fourth, leaders shape culture by what they praise and what they rebuke. If leaders celebrate baptisms, the church will learn to value baptisms. Leaders get to define "the win." Define this carefully, because if you value the wrong thing as a leader, the church may follow. If evangelism is praised and gossip rebuked by the leadership, the members will begin viewing evangelism and gossip in ways consistent with those actions.

Fifth, leaders shape culture through personal example. A church is unlikely to develop a culture of mission involvement if the leaders of the church never go on mission trips themselves. Leading by example is one of the most powerful ways to shape the culture of the church. Servant leadership encourages others to serve. Missional leadership encourages others to be mission-minded. To be a disciple is to be a "learner." The teacher can shape the behavior,

To be a disciple is to be a "learner."

values, and beliefs of the learner in significant ways through example. So whatever you want to see in the congregation must be clearly modeled!

Sixth, leaders shape culture through the power of persuasive personal influence. There is an interesting theme in Luke's gospel. There are great moments of influence that occur in the context of hospitality and meals. One of my favorite examples of this is the story of Zacchaeus. After eating together and being around Jesus one-on-one, Zacchaeus pledged to give half of his possessions to the poor and pay back four times what he extorted from others. If you are a leader, don't underestimate the persuasive power of your personal influence. Just a word of caution, someone is always watching you!

Just a word of caution, someone is always watching you!

The Power of Community

A final method for shaping the culture of your church is through the power of community. There is a tipping point at which people in the church will adapt to change, and the tipping point is when they see people in the church that they trust support the vision. Researchers call these people "key stakeholders," those who hold influence over others in the organization. Peer influence is powerful in shaping culture. This is why church discipline is so powerful, as an example.

If you can connect with the key stakeholders in your church, you can help change the culture. In the church in which I was raised, the youth group had an contagious passion for music. One of the reasons for this (beyond other cultural elements in our church such as an annual worship conference) was that the teenagers who were popular leaders played instruments or were singers. This had a profound impact on others who looked up to these individuals. Church staff, deacons, small group leaders, and other lay leaders can help lead innovative change by using the power of their collective voice in making the change initiative turn from an individual vision (that of the pastor) to a community vision.

In the New Testament, the early church understood the power of community influence. At the Jerusalem Council, for instance, "the apostles and elders, with the whole church" used their collective voice to influence the church at Antioch (Acts 15:22). When the church at Antioch received a letter from Jerusalem with instructions, "they rejoiced because of its encouragement" (Acts 15:31). I believe one of the reasons the Jerusalem letter was so effective was because it carried the weight of the entire community. A church's culture develops only when it develops broadly throughout the entire body. Therefore, to change the culture of your church, you need for it to be widespread throughout the membership. Learn to use the power of others in persuading the church to adapt to a vision or change initiative. Only when the entire community adapts has there been an actual change in the culture of the Church.

For so many years, the emphasis in church leadership research has been on church growth methodologies. There has been much good that has come as a result of the conferences, books, and leaders that this movement has produced. Yet, one of the church growth movement's leaders, Bill Hybels, acknowledged a few years ago that while the church has learned how to increase attendance, it still lacks health in many ways.

The conversation that the next generation of leaders must have is how to ensure church health. My belief is that the most effective way of creating healthy churches is to create church cultures that reflect Biblical norms. Until we produce a culture of excellence, leadership, evangelism and discipleship in our churches, for instance, we will never have healthy churches, regardless of whether our services have a crowd or not. Wise leaders will learn to understand and shape the culture of their churches to reflect faithfulness to the Scripture.

"When Alexander the Great lay dying, they asked him, 'Whose is the kingdom?' And he replied, 'It is for him who can take it!' It will be we, or somebody else." The future of the church lies in wait for those who will take it. The Lord graces us with the opportunity to lead His people. Leaders who shape their church's culture in ways that are faithful to His Word will bring much glory to God and great benefit to the kingdom. Let's decide now to take territory and influence for our King!

DR. MARTIN WILLIAMS

CHAPTER
4

DR. MARTIN WILLIAMS

Ignorant Gatekeepers

Experiences shape perceptions.

~ Dr. Samuel Chand

2 Kings 7:1-2 Then Elisha said, "Hear the word of the Lord. Thus says the Lord: 'Tomorrow about this time a seah of fine flour shall be sold for a shekel, and two seahs of barley for a shekel, at the gate of Samaria.'" 2 So an officer on whose hand the king leaned answered the man of God and said, "Look, if the Lord would make windows in heaven, could this thing be? "And he said, "In fact, you shall see it with your eyes, but you shall not eat of it."

Honestly, this is one of my most favorite stories in the Bible, because it fully encapsulates the idea of this book. It has so many overtones, undertones, types, shadows and the like that it would be very difficult to miss the driving points of God's heart.

Let's give a bit of background. The Syrian King Ben-Hadad decided to besiege the Israelites in Samaria, surround it and starve them out. Obviously the king would need a long-term plan to get this done. Eventually the city was in dire straits, meaning economically everything inside the city was chaotic and financially bankrupt. There was no food and no water. It was so bad that it came down to the point where an actual donkey's head was sold for a fortune. People were even buying pigeon dung and boiling it to make soup for eating. This was a really bad situation.

Worst of all was when the king heard this sad story in his kingdom. There were two women who lived together that were so hungry they made a pact to eat their young children. The first woman gave up her son to eat him, and when the time came for the second woman to give up her son she ran and hid him. This obviously broke the king's heart. He even tore off his robe and wept in front of his kingdom. Imagine with me that this was a really bad situation.

Elijah, the prophet, was at his house when the king sent a messenger. This messenger wanted him to know that the king blamed him for his turmoil. Elijah had a prophecy for them. His prophecy was that in 24 hours everything would shift. What is interesting is that he actually predicted that the shift would happen at the gate of Samaria.

Absolutely nothing is going right in this city. There was hunger everywhere. The prophet predicts a total turnaround in 24 hours. That in itself is interesting but he also predicts where it's going to happen. He says that

The gate is the place of "transfer".

the gate will be the place of this miraculous turnaround.

Remember, the gate is the place of transactions. The gate is the place of entrance. The gate is the place of "transfer". A place where ruling authorities occupy making decisions for those housed inside the city gates. Most importantly don't forget that Jacob called the House of God "the gate." The type and shadow here is that no matter what is going on in the world around us a shift can happen overnight through the Church. So don't get worried about earthly government because as I have said earlier, our government is not of this world. And as long as we are Kingdom citizens, we will always be covered.

It is also important to notice that the king leaned on the hand of a man. In other words the king trusted a man, that he depended on and evidently gave ear to this man's judgment. This man was in charge of the gate. Like the ten spies that Moses sent out to the Promised Land, who returned with a negative report, his judgment of God's word was negative. He couldn't believe it. So he openly made a negative comment. He said "that even if God was involved, if He opened the windows of Heaven this would never happen." What a huge leadership flaw! This could be one of major problems with the Church today, the senior leader is relying on congregational leaders that are not in agreement with the set man.

The king in this Scripture is a type of Christ. He has put his trust in the Church that He has instituted. The body of Christ standing as one man in the earth is how God wanted the Church. Jesus' original plan was for the gate to be the Church. What happens when the Church becomes unconscious to its assignment? What happens when the Church is oblivious to its calling? What happens when the Church is more concerned about religion than a relationship with God? What happens when the Church has the wrong concept of their original responsibility?

What happened in this story is still happening to the Church today. You can recollect the story; there were four lepers who were outside the gate of Samaria. They didn't have a Church, they didn't hear the prophecy, and they were not allowed to be in the city for any reason. But somehow they asked the question, "why should we sit here and die?" That question changed everything. It opened up their lives to possibilities and the city for rescue. I am convinced that even though things in life can be really bad that it does not take a senate to provoke change – just a few people who decide to stick together and walk in agreement can change the destiny for a nation.

Remember that these lepers ended up in the camp of the Syrians, where they found food and water to feed the whole city for months. These lepers reacted on a word they did not hear. They made a conscious connection to an unconscious revelation, which the Church and the man in charge of the gate decided to ignore. Remember, God is always speaking but are we always listening? Maybe if we stop just praying, just shouting and start believing in what we are praying we too would hear! This is a serious component of a believer's life that needs to be activated. We must pray but at some point, we must get up and act on what we believe.

Remember, God is always speaking but are we always listening?

Elijah's word to the gatekeeper is piercing, shocking and overwhelmingly convicting. He tells him that even though he's in charge of the gate and should receive full benefit of his assignment, he will literally see the turnaround at his gate but not be able to eat of it. He would witness it with his eyes but never taste it with his lips. He would see others

— experience what he should have

experienced first. He would watch others

*Expecting
should lead to
receiving.* benefit from his calling but never get the

joy of it himself. This is sad! The Church

can get into a position where it has so much belief that it

never uses its faith. Expecting should lead to receiving. So,

let's see how this ends.

> *2 Kings 7:16-18 Then the people went out and plundered the tents of the Syrians. So a seah of fine flour was sold for a shekel, and two seahs of barley for a shekel, according to the word of the Lord. 17 Now the king had appointed the officer on whose hand he leaned to have charge of the gate. But the people trampled him in the gate, and he died, just as the man of God had said, who spoke when the king came down to him. 18 So it happened just as the man of God had spoken to the king, saying, "Two seahs of barley for a shekel, and a seah of fine flour for a shekel, shall be sold tomorrow about this time in the gate of Samaria."*

When the lepers went back to the city and told the gatekeepers that the Syrian army had fled and left all of their supplies they did not believe them. The gatekeepers sent spies out to see if the lepers were telling the truth. When they were found to be telling the truth everyone in the city rushed out to the Syrian camp and begin to plunder.

They even followed them for miles and there was more plunder.

The man, who was in charge of the gate, that the Bible says the king leaned on his hand, was standing inside the gate when all of these people came back with barley and wheat. But he never got to taste the barley and wheat because he was trampled by the people coming back into the city. At the end of the story the full prophecy of Elijah was true down to the very last word.

Just a few more questions, "Have you ever thought much about God leaning on the Church? Have you considered the fact that God is depending on the Church? What if He is? What condition do you think the Church is in? Do we still see ourselves as the gate, the place where miracles can happen? Do we see that God could give us more than enough and we could feed the nations? Just how do we see our role as the Church? Overall, how we see ourselves is an indicator of our level of effectiveness! But why was this man, the one the king was leaning on? I don't know maybe the guy once was engaged with the vision and somehow after time, he lost his passion to serve. But I do know this is a major problem in most churches.

Leaders are the future hope of the Church.

45

In order to be a healthy church, every senior pastor must have faithful leaders who understand the vision. "Leaders are the future hope of the Church." Who among us with any local church experience would disagree? I'm not aware of any church that would post a sign on its marquee out front announcing, "No leaders needed!" So why don't churches develop leaders? The number one reason is that most simply do not know how. Also, many churches simply do not have the time. It is difficult, if not impossible, for the senior pastor to find the time as well as have the expertise to develop and maintain such a vital process--especially in a large church. Secondly, if you leave their development up to the leaders themselves, it may be sporadic at best, if it happens at all. A third is that Satan does not want churches to develop leaders because of the positive impact such a process will have in promoting and expanding God's kingdom.

2 Timothy 2:1-2 You then, my son, be strong in the grace that is in Christ Jesus. 2 And the things you have heard me say in the presence of many witnesses entrust to reliable people who will also be qualified to teach others.

As a leader one of your responsibilities is to steer the congregation in following God's design and purposes for the Church. This is accomplished by modeling it in your own ministry, by structuring for it to happen and by equipping other leaders to align themselves with God.

Just as the varying parts of the human body need each other to best accomplish its work, so the Body of Christ needs to function interdependently, like a team. (Romans 12:4-8; 1 Corinthians 12:12-27). God so designed the Church that it "grows and builds itself up in love, as each part does its work" (Ephesians. 4:16).

CHAPTER
5

DR. MARTIN WILLIAMS

The Unconscious Church

You're not looking for solutions, you are the solution!
~Dr. Martin Williams

Jesus was talking to His disciples one day and He decided to describe the condition of how He saw the Church. He gave a great depiction of what the Church was like in His generation. Let's read what He said:

> *Matthew 11:16-19 "But to what shall I liken this generation? It is like children sitting in the marketplaces and calling to their companions, 17 and saying: 'We played the flute for you, And you did not dance; We mourned to you, And you did not lament.' 18 For John came neither eating nor drinking, and they say, 'He has a demon.' 19 The Son of Man came eating and drinking, and they say, 'Look, a glutton and a winebibber, a friend of tax collectors and sinners!' But wisdom is justified by her children."*

Jesus's statement is conceptual but very practical. He says the Church is like children who were in a place of transfer referred to as the marketplace, and while there in this place of transfer they were playing games. The marketplace during Jesus's day was located immediately inside the gate. The gate was the entrance to the city; it is where elders sat and judged what came in and out of the city and it was also the marketplace. At the gate of the city the elders acted like "watchmen" and like a clearing house for access. The elders primary duty was to approve what would be allowed to enter the city.

I'll never forget the time years ago when I needed to go inside the bank to do some personal business. When I got to the bank there was a line of people waiting to get to the counter to allow the teller to help them. In one of the lines was a mother with two children. I take for granted they were her children because she was trying to discipline them with her voice and get them to act properly. They seemed to be between the ages of seven and nine. Even though she was trying to discipline them and direct them with her voice they were not listening at all. They were tearing the magazines, overflowing the water fountain and running around the coffee tables. At times the kids even accidently ran over other people in the bank. If the lines had not been so long she would have probably been out of there in five minutes. But that day that wasn't the case for her.

After waiting like me, she found out she was in the wrong line and that she needed to sit and wait for a loan officer. This woman had been walking to work for several weeks not to mention she probably had many challenges getting the kids where they needed to be during the week. She came to the bank that day to try to get a loan for a car. Her children being young did not understand that this was one of the most important meetings of the week for their family. And also like children, they didn't understand that by having a car it would change their lives by allowing the mother to get back and forth to work as well as getting them to their appointments. They made so much noise and became such a distraction that when the loan officer came out to meet with her she was in tears and left the bank without talking to him.

Have you ever had to take your children with you while doing serious business? How did they behave? Were you able to get your work done? Was it hard to stay focused? Do you recall the reason why the children were with you in this type of setting? I think we all can somewhat identify with a day like the one I just described.

That's how Jesus felt when He was on earth. He felt like

the people in the gate which actually represent the Church did not understand the concept of the marketplace. They could not grasp the importance of being gatekeepers. The Church was simply unconscious to the concept of things shifting, switching and turning around through the Church. Do you have that concept of Church? The Church is the place of transfer. According to God, the Church will always be the most important entity on the planet!

Just consider the heart break that Jesus must have felt as He observed the condition of the generation that He was sent to birth His Church through. Can you imagine what Jesus was thinking?

The generation was **unconscious**.

Unconsciousness happens when a part of the mind is inaccessible to the conscious mind and affects behavior and emotions. The people of that era had lost their access to the assignment given to the

—

Can you imagine what Jesus was thinking?

people of God to rule and reign on the earth. This state of mind affected them emotionally and most of all it effected their actions. They behaved as though the life around them was a game. They were not operating as if they were God's called-out people with purpose.

It seems that they spent most of their time manipulating

one another instead of leading in society. Breaking the heart of God they were no longer aware of what was happening around them. They were **unaware** that they were sitting in a place of the transfer of power.

The generation was **undefined** in the sense that their original design and assignment was not settled. The specifics of God's instructions and destiny for them had been put aside and forgotten. God had made His plans specific and very clear to His people. So how had they allowed life to dull their senses in such a way? When the Church loses its' heart of purpose, it loses everything.

Do you have that concept of Church?

The people of that generation were **unprepared**. Specifically they were not ready for the work at hand. Their ability to deal with the challenges of the times was beyond them. The religious system of the day did not even understand Jesus' message. This is a fact proven by their desire and plan to rid themselves of His voice. They weren't ready for His mind. They weren't ready for His message and they weren't ready for His mission.

When you are not ready for a thing you will probably not be willing to participate. A person who has spent no time and effort in preparation will be reluctant to participate in the process. This is where the Church found itself in the days and times of Jesus.

> *Ephesians 2:10 For we are God's workmanship, created in Christ Jesus to do good works, which God prepared in advance for us to do.*

This speaks to the next point, the generation was simply **unengaged**. The people of God were not employed any longer by their Master. This is obvious by the way they served the vision of the One, Who gave birth to them. People who are not engaged will never fully occupy. They will not advance. They will never

— We have no excuse not to be productive.

take territory. They will never conquer. As a matter of fact, they will not even know that they should be doing exploits.

Occupying for the King will only be done by those who understand the reason for their assignment. Salt in the shaker may be powerful but in reality it is impotent until it is put into action outside the shaker.

The Church has been chosen to be in the world influencing it and expanding the Kingdom of God.

> *Luke 9:62 But Jesus said to him, "No one, having put his hand to the plow, and looking back, is fit for the kingdom of God."*

Naturally any people who are unconscious, undefined, unprepared and unengaged will be **unproductive**. Unproductivity is a result of not working and getting results. Work is a response to one's assignment. Assignment comes from someone who you are submitted to. The people of God are unproductive because we are not submitted to the Kingship of Christ. The

The people of God are unproductive because we are not submitted to the Kingship of Christ.

Scripture has stated that we are to be about our Father's business and that we should be doing "greater" works.

We have been given the authority and power to do exploits. We have no excuse not to be productive. We are children of the Most High and He is expecting us to produce. Jesus ended this discourse by saying that wisdom will be justified by its children. Wisdom is proven by what it produces.

Children and the Church are a direct reflection of where they came from.

John 14:12-14 "Most assuredly, I say to you, he who believes in Me, the works that I do he will do also; and greater works than these he will do, because I go to My Father. 13 And whatever you ask in My name, that I will do, that the Father may be glorified in the Son. 14 If you ask anything in My name, I will do it.
If the Church can catch hold of its true assignment, we

will be justified by what we produce. In other words, as children of God we are not to behave like the children in the bank. We are to operate in wisdom because we came out of God and our heavenly Father is full of wisdom. Children and the Church are a direct reflection of where they came from.

CHAPTER
6

DR. MARTIN WILLIAMS

The World is the Lord's

Foolish people haven't realized that God owns everything.
~Dr. Martin Williams

It's a good time in this book to remind everyone that all is not lost. No matter what has happened, no matter what decision Adam made or what we believe Adam lost. This verse in Psalms reminds us of something very important:

Psalm 24:1 The earth is the Lord's, and all its fullness, the world and those who dwell therein.

The earth is the Lord's. All the dirt on the planet, all the territory, every tree, all of it belongs to the Lord. All of the fullness of the earth belongs to the Lord.

— *The earth is the Lord's.*

That is everything that comes out of the ground, every

animal. All of the air belongs to the Lord.

He then says the world belongs to the Lord. Worlds are systems on the planet. It is the systems that make the earth habitable.

Lastly, David declares that the people in the worlds don't necessarily live on the earth, they really live in systems on the earth. If it were not for these worlds people could not live on the earth. These worlds include water systems, air systems, food systems, governmental systems, educational systems, law systems and economic systems.

My point with Psalm 24 is this; everything that God created and gave to Adam to rule over in the Garden of Eden still exists. Every world that Adam had dominion over has not been destroyed, they are simply in the wrong hands. The Church has been given this duty to operate in Adam's absence. The baton has been safely passed on to mankind to continue will of God on earth.

The Church has been given this duty to operate in Adam's absence.

These worlds, systems and kingdoms were created for Adam. The intent was for him to use them to manage the earth. Whatever Adam abdicated through his personal ignorance, God still possesses and intends for the Church to manage.

For example, God created the world of government. This is the world that manages people, ensures justice, and maintains order inside a nation. It was always God's intent that this world be managed and governed by the Church.

—

It was always God's intent that this world be managed and governed by the Church.

Proverbs 29:2 When the righteous are in authority, the people rejoice; But when a wicked man rules, the people groan.

Remember we already reviewed in a previous chapters that God chose to use the Church as the gate where earth would have access to Heaven. So the Church would be the only one on earth to know God's will. They would be the ones judging what is right and what is wrong. They would ensure that there is justice and peace, but at some point in history, the Church lost this revelation and became corrupted.

It is obvious that the world of government is no longer in the hands of the Church. You need only to turn on the television to see the evidence of inequality, injustice, and corruption in every government. Yet this world is not lost. It is simply in the wrong hands, waiting for the Church to take it back.

Romans 8:19-22 For the earnest expectation of the creation eagerly waits for the revealing of the sons of God. 20 For the creation was subjected to futility, not willingly, but because of Him who subjected it in hope; 21 because the creation itself also will be delivered from the bondage of corruption into the glorious liberty of the children of God. 22 For we know that the whole creation groans and labors with birth pangs together until now.

These verses mean something totally different in this new revelation. It means that the world of government was subjected to being lost. It didn't want to be lost and these verses also say that it will be delivered back into the hands of the rightful owners - the Church.

Let's Make a Deal

This brings me to the beautiful story of Jesus's testing and His calling. Most people fail to understand what the testing of Jesus was all about. Most people think it was just the devil testing Him before He went into ministry. It's very common to hear that Jesus was being tested in the lust of His flesh, lust of His eyes and the pride of His life. I really think all of these are true but there is a deeper meaning to the testing of Jesus. Let's read the scriptural account.

Matthew 4:8-11 Again, the devil took Him up on an

exceedingly high mountain, and showed Him all the kingdoms of the world and their glory. 9 And he said to Him, "All these things I will give You if You will fall down and worship me." 10 Then Jesus said to him, "Away with you, Satan! For it is written, 'You shall worship the Lord your God, and Him only you shall serve.'" 11 Then the devil left Him, and behold, angels came and ministered to Him.

Jesus had fasted food and water for 40 days, spending time with the Father and time in preparation for ministry. At the end of the 40 days the devil came; he was called the tempter. The first thing he tempted Jesus with was His hunger. He asked Him to turn stones into bread. Jesus's defense was both scriptural and pointed. Jesus said, "get thee behind me"!

The next test he gave Jesus was to jump from the top of the temple to the ground to see if God would protect Him. Perhaps he wanted to see how close God and Jesus really were in covenant. Perhaps he was just being ridiculous. I honestly think it was that he was just being cunning as is his true nature. We will clearly know what he really wanted in the third challenge or temptation he presented to Jesus.

Spiritually Jesus was taken to the place where He could have a supernatural view of the kingdoms of this world. He wanted Jesus to be reminded of the world systems. As I said before, God made it very clear that the world still belongs to Him, that every system created in Genesis belonged to Him. They are the Lord's. They will always belong to God.

It would seem that if satan said to Jesus that all the systems of the world were his that Jesus would have challenged him. Surprisingly Jesus did not. You know the reason why Jesus did not challenge satan? Because satan was actually telling the truth. The world and its systems were in satan's hands even though he did not own rightfully own them. They were abdicated into his hands in Genesis 3 when Adam was removed from Eden. So when we just sit back and don't operate in our full God-given authority, we continue to abdicate. It is very clear in the Word of God that He has commanded us to go into the world and into every system and occupy. God's desire is that we do business for His Kingdom!

Everything on the earth was touched, managed and controlled from the Garden of Eden.

Remember Eden was that place that Adam ruled the world from. A river went out from Adam that watered the entire earth. Everything on the earth was touched, managed and controlled from the Garden of Eden.

Now Jesus is being challenged and satan knew exactly

what Jesus wanted. But satan wanted something too; he wanted to be worshiped as God. He wanted Jesus to serve him. What would Jesus's answer be?

Just imagine for a moment you as a creator. You have created the systems that rule the world. Someone has them but they didn't create them, and now they're trying to sell them back to you, but they want your soul for it. However, satan has one problem that he hasn't thought about. Jesus has no ability to worship him. In this sense Jesus's knees can never bow to satan. I think you and I should have the same inability. We must never bow to him or worship him.

Jesus's answer was simple. If I accept these worlds back from you, then I will have to worship you. There is no way that Jesus can worship satan, an angel that He created. Jesus reminds him that it's God and God alone that He will worship!

DR. MARTIN WILLIAMS

CHAPTER
7

DR. MARTIN WILLIAMS

No, I'll Use My Church

We don't have to make the Bible relevant –it always was.
~Dr. Rick Warren

Tons of questions go through my mind as Jesus has just denied satan by not worshiping him. Jesus held His integrity but it still seems like the world that He created is lost in the hands of satan forever. Do you believe that God would be satisfied with everything He created in satan's hands for eternity? No! I don't either. It would be difficult to call God wise if that was the case. He's not just wise, He is wisdom. There is no way anyone can challenge God. No one can teach God. No one can counsel God.

No one can counsel God.

He simply stands alone in His own sovereignty and His power and wisdom. Whatever God wanted in the beginning He's going to have before it's over. Let's remind ourselves of what He wanted from the beginning.

God wanted dominion on earth without having to live on earth, through His spiritual children. He wanted to rule the world, not be in charge of the world, but be able to rule it through His offspring. God's original heart was that you and I would be His true representation in the earth.

Whatever God wanted in the beginning is what He will have when the end comes.

He wanted to form a dynasty of children. He wanted a different territory called earth to be ruled by His sons and daughters. Whatever God wanted in the beginning is what He will have when the end comes.

So what was God's plan to get His world back? Let's read and find out.

> *Matthew 16:13-19 When Jesus came into the region of Caesarea Philippi, He asked His disciples, saying, "Who do men say that I, the Son of Man, am?" 14 So they said, "Some say John the Baptist, some Elijah, and others Jeremiah or one of the prophets." 15 He said to them, "But who do you say that I am?" 16 Simon Peter answered and said, "You are the Christ, the Son of the living God." 17 Jesus answered and said to him, "Blessed are you, Simon Bar-Jonah, for flesh and blood has not revealed this to you, but My Father who is in heaven. 18 And I also say to you that you are Peter, and on this rock I will build My church, and the gates of Hades shall not prevail against it. 19 And I*

will give you the keys of the kingdom of heaven, and whatever you bind on earth will be bound in heaven, and whatever you loose on earth will be loosed in heaven."

It was a very legitimate question for Jesus to ask His disciples around Him, "Who do men say that I am?" Surely His disciples would know the chatter around town. After all their families would be giving their opinions to the inhabitants of the towns that they traveled to. Maybe their answers to Him was a bit of a surprise. None of the people in the cities they visited believed that Jesus was the Messiah. They simply saw Him as a prophet.

The second question, however, is a bit more surprising. Jesus had not told the disciples who He was. Jesus had not told them that He was the promised King. So when He asked them, "Who do you think I am?" all they had to judge was His words and His works. His words because they were only words that a king could make and His works because it would be impossible to do the things Jesus did without power from a higher source.

However, it was Peter that got revelation by the Holy Spirit that Jesus was the Christ. That Jesus was the promised King that would come, the One that would restore dominion to Israel. By revelation Peter said He was God's

Son. This was more revelation to them than it is to us because this was the first time they'd heard it. Jesus is God's Son that He promised would come to be the Messiah and return the Kingdom to Israel. Amazingly this had to have shaken the disciples to the core.

God has one pattern, and we must build according to His pattern.

It seemed as equally exciting to Jesus, as if He had been waiting for this revelation for eternity. For indeed He had been waiting at least since the day Adam fell.

God has one plan: to call out a people from all nations to be called by His name. God has one pattern, and we must build according to His pattern. His plan brings us to His end purpose; therefore we cannot lay it aside and bring in our own plan. Man's ways may look good for a time, but God's wisdom is revealed for eternity. In a true expression of the Body of Christ, the basis of gathering is the life of God; the purpose of gathering is to be made one and to contain the fullness of Christ; and, the order of gathering is in faith, directed by the Holy Spirit. We must see the Church for what it is through Christ Jesus.

Man's ways may look good for a time, but God's wisdom is revealed for eternity.

When Jesus said, "I will build my church," what did He mean? Many movements of our day are trying to build the kingdom of God with natural authority. With a lack of spiritual understanding and discernment, we may start from our own experience and build on that. But Jesus said that if we want to build on the rock, we must hear God first, then act on what we hear. We need to know what God is really doing in this hour--how His plan works out in believers' lives.

God's purpose encompasses many things, but His ultimate goal is to bring us into perfect oneness with Himself. The purpose of God is God Himself, and for us to move in this purpose, we first must see it by the Spirit. His plan is perfectly designed to bring us into His purpose. Within God's plan, He has an order--for the family, for the Church, and for our lives. Now that this revelation is realized Jesus can put His plan into action.

The purpose of God is God Himself

Here are the components of this revelation:

Those who received this revelation are blessed. Let's face it, everyone doesn't have this revelation because it takes relationship with God to understand the Church's role in society. Most in the world believe that the Church is here just to feed the hungry, visit people in prison or simply to — get people saved and prepared for heaven.

He is and was the King promised to return by God When you receive the revelation that Jesus is not only Savior and Lord but He's also King; that changes everything! My prayer is that you received this revelation that Jesus is the Christ. He is and was the King promised to return by God in Genesis 3.

You must receive and embrace this truth. I also believe that many of you received this from the Father by the Holy Spirit. It could not possibly only be that Peter had head knowledge of this truth; it had to be revealed by the Holy Spirit. I pray this enters your spirit and becomes part of your life. From this day forward it should be your motivation to receive the actual heart of God about who Jesus is and what He did.

This revelation is the bedrock for Jesus' plan. The reason this revelation is so important is because it will become the actual foundation for understanding the Church. Those who don't get this revelation will be on shaky ground. They will live with the misconception of how important the church is to the world. In God's eyes the

Church was created to save the world and every system that manages the world. Having a clear revelation of the Church and your role is crucial for God's plan to succeed.

I will build My Church. Jesus promises that on this very deep and stable foundation He will construct His Church. Let me reiterate how important this revelation is. Jesus did not say He would build "a" church, He said that He would build "the" Church. This is significant, because only kings in those days had churches. The Greek word is ecclesia. An ecclesia is a group of people who were called-out to represent the king in important matters. Through this group called the ecclesia or church, the king's will would be executed. These are people who have His heart and know His will. They are also given permission to act on His behalf. That's why this revelation of Jesus being King is so important. He wasn't just a man of flesh; He was and is King! Jesus had full authority to appoint the Church as His earthly representation to the world. The Church should know and always be ready to execute the heart of God in the world. He promised to build His Church and construct it for His

Having a clear revelation of the Church and your role is crucial for God's plan to succeed.

purposes alone. If you and I are part of the Church that God has called out, it should be our priority to execute His perfect will. The Church is a serious entity not a if-you-feel-like joining this Sunday kind of attitude. The Church is the most important institution on the planet. The Church is God's only vehicle in getting His will done on earth!

Hell's gates will not be able to resist. Then Jesus makes this most important promise. It's a promise we've been waiting for, for over 4,000 years. That the systems that satan took and locked behind his gates would finally be returned to the saints by access through the Church. This is God's plan. All of these systems and the world will be brought back to God by His Church. This would position the Church as the gatekeeper again in accordance to God's original plan. Jesus did not bow to satan and serve him for these kingdoms. He decided He would get them back through the Church. In fact, the Gates of Hell that guarded and protected the systems will no longer have power. Then satan would be totally powerless against the Church. And again the kingdoms of this world would become the kingdoms of our Lord and His Christ.

The Church is God's only vehicle in getting His will done on earth!

I will give My Church the keys of Heaven. And Hell's gate will not be able to resist us. Jesus will give us the authority to manage the earth again. Keys describe access, agreement, permission, control, management and power. These keys of the earth according to Jesus would be given to His Church; not necessarily to individuals, but to this collective group of called-out representatives referred to as the "ecclesia". These are heavenly keys and the keys to manage earth; keys made in Heaven giving us access to have dominion over the planet. It's one thing to have a key to the house – it's another thing to have the key to all the doors in the house. What God has done through Jesus Christ is given this multiplicity of keys to the earth and to the church. It is important to note that He says keys not just one key. The earth is not one-dimensional, it is multifaceted. There are many systems, or kingdoms, on this earth,

Keys describe access, agreement, permission, control, management and power.

The Church has a huge responsibility in accepting the —keys!

all made by God to be managed by man. Jesus at His death, burial and resurrection restored these keys to mankind not to rule over one another but to rule the earth and its systems. The Church has a huge responsibility in accepting the keys! Remember, one of the main Kingdom principles in being restored back to our place of authority through the finished work of Jesus is proper management.

Whatever the Church does not permit on earth I will not permit in Heaven. Please do not overlook the fact that these keys have been given to the Church. Once God gave us the keys the authority was given to us. With authority comes responsibility. With responsibility comes accountability. With accountability comes management.

With responsibility comes accountability.

Lastly, with management comes reward or punishment. With the keys in our hands we are solely responsible. This means God does not have total control. This means He has abdicated His control. He has delegated His control. What we permit, God's permits. We have a very important role in restoring the kingdom and worldly systems back to God.

What we permit, God's permits.

For clarity let's understand that Heaven is the headquarters and that whatever the Church permits must have already been originally acceptable to God. We do not have the right to disallow something on earth that heaven doesn't agree with. Remember, we are His Church. If earth is a mess, it is a mess that we have tolerated or created. If earth has problems, they are problems that we allow. If earth is mismanaged, it is mismanagement that we permitted. I think it's time that we realize that there are some things we should not allow. Furthermore, it is way past time that as believers we step up and activate our power to do something about this mess we are responsible for on earth.

We are responsible for the generations to come and it's our duty to do our best to get this chaos under control and managed.

We are responsible for the generations to come and it's our duty to do our best to get this chaos under control and managed.

Whatever the Church allows on earth I will allow in Heaven. Conversely, what the Church thinks is right to allow Heaven backs up. The Church is ordained to have meetings, sing, pray and preach and disciple those outside the Covenant.

After we exit Church we must learn how to be the Church.

After we exit Church we must learn how to be the Church. This multifaceted, multifunctional entity has only bright spots and no ignorance; this is the Church.

DR. MARTIN WILLIAMS

CHAPTER
8

DR. MARTIN WILLIAMS

What Is the Church?

Pastors are the most strategic change agents to deal with the
problem in society.
~Dr. Rick Warren

It is important that we clarify the meanings of words for the
sake of understanding and communication. When we say
the word church, it conjures up lots of concepts in people's
minds.

To some the church is a place to get married and buried.
To others it is a social club to meet people and have
friends. Unfortunately some see the church as a place of
prestige where they get status from. I was awfully surprised
when one person told me that they were looking for a
church that would give them contacts for their business.

In Matthew 16:18 Jesus said,

"And I also say to you that you are Peter, and on this rock I will build My church, and the gates of Hades shall not prevail against it."

In this process of building brilliant churches, it is important for us to determine and make connection with the mind of Jesus. The Greek word for the word church in this Scripture is "ecclesia." Jesus used this word three times in His teaching sessions and they are only recorded in the book of Matthew.

In Strong's Greek Concordance, the word ecclesia is defined as "an assembly" which is from the word "ek" which means "out of" and the word "klesis" which means "a calling." So in simple terms, ecclesia means to be "called out to be an assembly." So that's exactly what the church is, a people who have been called out to make an assembly. The One, Who has chosen and called us out is Jesus, according to John 15:16.

"You did not choose Me, but I chose you and appointed you that you should go and bear fruit, and that your fruit should remain, that whatever you ask the Father in My name He may give you."

Additionally, according to this Scripture we also get a glimpse of the why He called us out. He has an expectation of us producing fruit that lasts through eternity.

Are you excited? I know I am. He even goes on to promise that whatever we need to produce this fruit that lasts that He will give it to us. God has and always will be faithful to His Word! The next important thing to understand and acknowledge is what He called us out of and what He has delivered us from. It is very clear as noted in Isaiah 52:11:

> *"Depart! Depart! Go out from there, Touch no unclean thing; Go out from the midst of her, Be clean, You who bear the vessels of the Lord."*

When we look at the original language, the phrase "Go out from the midst of her" it is translated "go out from the center." And the word "her" is translated "self." Basically, what this is saying is that we should depart or separate ourselves from our self-will and also from any forms of self-righteousness. We should no longer seek after the center of our longing and focus in life but on the center of His longing and whatever is pleasing and acceptable unto Him.

And if you are part of the Church it means that God has called you to give up

To be clear, once you are saved, you are now part of the

Church. And if you are part of the Church it means that God has called you to give up yourself and live for Him. Not to leave you ignorant, He makes this statement in Matthew 10:38-39:

And he who does not take his cross and follow after Me is not worthy of Me. 39 He who finds his life will lose it, and he who loses his life for My sake will find it.

Jesus assures those He calls that if they want to have a great life they are to give it up for His sake. Our King is perfect and righteous in all His ways. Amen? So don't struggle with this principle, give up and give in to the perfect will of the King; and watch life get better for you.

When we describe the Church we should say that it is not some willy nilly, flem-flam, disorganized mess. It an organized body of people who function under the authority of the Scripture, have a biblical leader, preach and teach, participate in the sacraments, disciples of covenant and have a local to global mission to accomplish. Without these attributes the organization is simply a typical organization. It is not a church and cannot perform as such. So, back to my original question; What is the Church?

I will use these seven words to describe what the Church is. The Church is God's...

Atmosphere – the Church is where the King sits and makes His abode. It is where His name is on earth. He lives and moves in the churches praise and worship. It is the place where He shares His heart, mind and will. This is where He can focus all of His attention because this assembly is totally focused on Him.

1 Kings 9:3 And the Lord said to him: "I have heard your prayer and your supplication that you have made before Me; I have consecrated this house which you have built to put My name there forever, and My eyes and My heart will be there perpetually.

Agreement – the Church is the place of agreement for the King. I'll never forget the first time I saw a movie about King Arthur's men and his round table. I was amazed on how this room was guarded and protected because it was in this room that King Arthur revealed his heart, fears and desires among trusted friends and loyalists. Throughout the movie there were incredible scenes showing how all King Arthur's men would assemble around the table and draw their swords in order to put them together as a show of their united strength and honor to the king's wishes. Well, that's sort of the picture here. When God reveals His desire to His Church He expects total honor and unwavering agreement.

Matthew 18:20 "Again I say to you that if two of you agree on earth concerning anything that they ask, it will be done for them by My Father in heaven. 20 For where two or three are gathered together in My name, I am there in the midst of them."

Amen – the Church is the King's "amen" on earth or "so let it be done." Our job as part of His Church is to engage ourselves in His plans and purposes. We have died to our own desires and have given ourselves totally to His will. When God speaks or we when we believe we have received directions from the Scriptures, we should quickly say, "so let it be done".

The Church is the King's "amen" on earth or "so let it be done."

Matthew 6:10 Your kingdom come. Your will be done On earth as it is in heaven.

Agenda – On earth the Church is the King's agenda. We are always on His mind because He carries out His agenda through us. He has decided to make His church His focus because it would be difficult to carry out His will if we don't know it. Jesus made sure that we would always be connected to His agenda

On earth the Church is the King's agenda.

by giving us the Holy Spirit.

John 16:15 He will glorify Me, for He will take of what is Mine and declare it to you. 15 All things that the Father has are Mine. Therefore I said that He will take of Mine and declare it to you.

Advancement – the Church has been given the charge to advance and expand His Kingdom. Jesus is very clear that He wants disciples. He has also made it clear that His will is for the Church to reproduce disciples in every nation. We must never forget that the entire earth, worlds and the people in the worlds belong to Him. He wants us to advance the knowledge of Him in the universe.

Mark 16:15 And He said to them, "Go into all the world and preach the gospel to every creature.

Adoration – the Church is the King's adoration and glory. When God and the world looks at the church and its work it should be glorious and worthy of the adoration of the King. God has a great hope of glory in us. It is His Church that will finally restore all things back to Him.

—

The Church is the King's adoration and glory.

Ephesians 1:19 the eyes of your understanding being enlightened; that you may know what is the hope of His calling, what are the riches of the glory of His inheritance in the saints, 19 and what is the exceeding greatness of His power toward us who believe, according to the working of His mighty power.

Anticipation – the King, Himself anticipates that day when all of His will has been accomplished through the Church; which is His called-out ones in the earth.

Romans 8:21 For the creation was subjected to futility, not willingly, but because of Him who subjected it in hope; 21 because the creation itself also will be delivered from the bondage of corruption into the glorious liberty of the children of God.

His Mystery Made Plain

Ephesians 3:13 To me, who am less than the least of all the saints, this grace was given, that I should preach among the Gentiles the unsearchable riches of Christ, 9 and to make all see what is the fellowship of the mystery, which from the beginning of the ages has been hidden in God who created all things through Jesus Christ; 10 to the intent that now the manifold wisdom of God might be made known by the church to the principalities and powers in the heavenly places, 11 according to the eternal purpose which He accomplished in Christ Jesus our Lord, 12 in whom we have boldness and access with confidence through faith in Him. 13 Therefore I ask that you do not lose heart at my tribulations for you, which is your glory.

The Apostle Paul was definitely not a puffed up person. There was no arrogance found in him. He was a man of simple, humble truth. While considering himself the least of all the saints, he also realized that he had a special grace. What is grace? Grace is simply the supernatural ability of God to get things accomplished.

—

Grace is simply the supernatural ability of God to get things accomplished.

Apostle Paul believed that he needed grace. He needed a heavenly anointing to get something across to us.

He called it a mystery. A mystery is something that has to be figured out or someone needs to inform you. He also says that there is a fellowship of this mystery which only a few had the revelation of. In Apostle Paul's age he considered himself a fellow in this commitment to make known this mystery. Apostle Paul felt like he was in charge of administrating this heavenly estate.

—

A mystery is something that has to be figured out or someone needs to inform you.

He also says that from the beginning this mystery has been hidden in God. For the reason of dispensation Apostle Paul says that this mystery has been concealed in God. Simply, the fullness of time had come. Jesus's death, burial and resurrection had ushered in a new season; the season of the Kingdom of God had arrived on earth.

Apostle Paul reminded us that all things were created by and through Jesus. Even the worlds were framed by Him. It was with good understanding why Jesus died on the cross. Jesus died on the cross to restore the Kingdom to mankind. So how does Paul describe it?

He said that God was intentional in this day and age to show how multifaceted His wisdom is. Most importantly, He decided to show the universe His wisdom through the Church. His wisdom is called manifold, many sided or many faceted. God's wisdom is not just deep but is wide and vast in dimensions.

We were never supposed to be confined to Sunday morning for two hours. The Church was designed to be at the top of every system and discipline of life.

The Church of the Lord Jesus Christ was never supposed to be one-dimensional. We were never supposed to be confined to Sunday morning for two hours. The Church was designed to be at the top of every system and discipline of life. The Church was originally designed to rule and reign over all the systems and mountains of the entire world.

Remember the earth is the Lord's and all the worlds that

94

are on the earth are the Lord's. He wants to reign over the worlds of business, education, family, entertainment, government and health, finances and as well as church.

Micah 4:12 "But in the last days it shall come to pass, that the mountain of the house of the Lord shall be established in the top of the mountains, and it shall be exalted above the hills; and people shall flow unto it. 2 And many nations shall come, and say, "Come let us go up to the mountain of the Lord, and to the house of the God of Jacob; and he will teach us of his ways, and we will walk in his paths:" for the law shall go forth of Zion; and the word of the Lord from Jerusalem.

According to Apostle Paul's revelation the Church is responsible for showing how brilliant God is. God's attempt to show His brilliance was to build His Church!

DR. MARTIN WILLIAMS

CHAPTER
9

DR. MARTIN WILLIAMS

Brilliance: What Does It Mean?

Diamonds are nothing more than chunks of coal that
endured pressure.
~Dr. Martin Williams

Brilliant describes something super bright, like intense
lights at a football stadium, a super sparkly diamond, or the
student who graduates from Harvard at age 13.

Brilliant comes from the Italian word brillare, to
"sparkle" like those bright lights, diamonds, and brainiac
kid. British people love to say things are "Brilliant!" in the
same way Americans say "Awesome!" Brilliant describes
anything sparkly, fabulous, or full of light. A bright color is
brilliant, too, like the brilliant orange of a setting sun.

Below are a few scenarios of how many of us define

people we consider to be brilliant. When you come up with a solution to something that others couldn't figure out, you are seen as brilliant. It doesn't have to be on the

—

Brilliant people solve problems.

scale of solving world hunger. It can be finding a new route that skips traffic or a better way to save money.

- Brilliant people solve problems. They don't just complain about the problems around them. They are solution-oriented. They recognize the problem and don't speak until they've figured it out.
- Brilliant people take the leap. They do what others only dream of. They step out and take risks!
- Brilliant people are striking and have a distinctive brightness.
- Brilliant people are those who stand for something larger than themselves.
- Brilliant people reflect the greatness and creativity of God.

Other words we use to describe brilliant and/or brilliance:

- very bright
- shining
- intense

- gifted
- talented
- first class
- impressive
- a diamond of brilliant cut

We will define brilliance simply as the effect of light engaging with an object.

From the beginning of our experience together, I have been proving through Scripture that God's original idea was leadership of the entire earth. Starting with Adam, God has ordained that from this portal or gate He would water, supply, lead and direct the systems of the earth.

Brilliant people are those who stand for something larger than themselves.

For my last chapter I will use the brilliant diamond to deliver my main point. The Church is the most important entity on planet earth; however, it must be "brilliant" to be effective. Let's explore the brilliant cut diamond.

A brilliant diamond is a diamond cut in a particular form with numerous facets so as to have exceptional brilliance. The shape resembles that of a cone and provides maximized light return through the top of the diamond.

Brilliance, or brightness, refers to the white light that is reflected back to the eye from the diamond. Light enters through the top of the diamond (the table), is broken down into a rainbow of spectral colors, and is reflected back and forth in the interior of the gem by bouncing off the mirror-like facets. Light exits through the table, recombining as white light.

The brilliant diamond is cut with seven intentional facets. These facets are designed to fully capture, embrace and emulate light when it engages with it. Please note that after the brilliant diamond engages light it is designed to reflect that light back out in the seven basic colors of the color spectrum.

—

The Church must be "brilliant" to be effective.

Seven facets intentionally cut to capture and reflect the seven different brilliant colors of light. As you are able to take a closer look at each of these unique colors, you will be totally amazed at how each carries their own color strength. For a colorful view, see diagrams:

martinwilliams.org/thebrilliantchurch

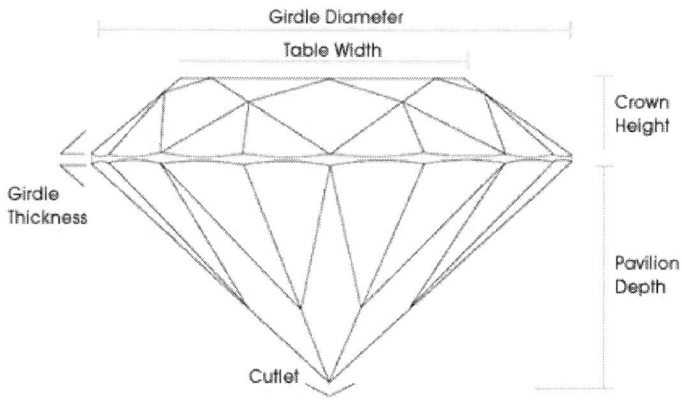

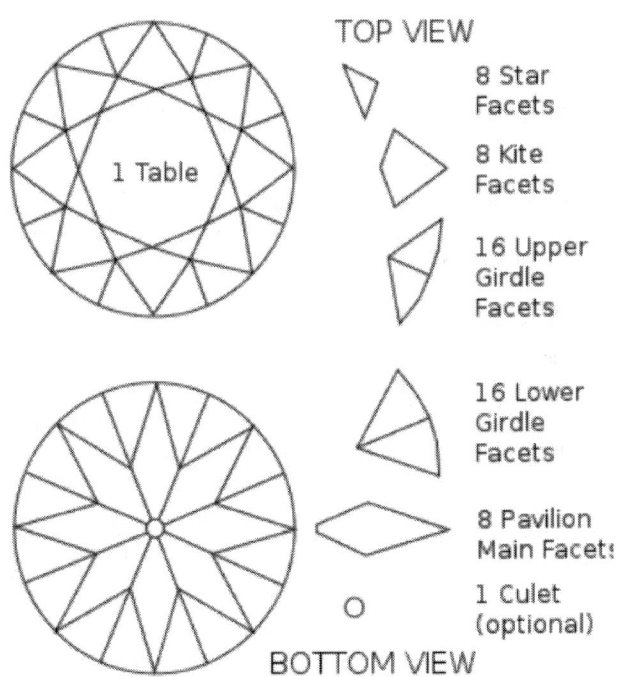

TOP VIEW

1 Table

8 Star Facets

8 Kite Facets

16 Upper Girdle Facets

16 Lower Girdle Facets

8 Pavilion Main Facets

1 Culet (optional)

BOTTOM VIEW

Let's make this plain; the brilliant diamond spends no time trying to create light. The brilliant diamond was purposely created to receive that light and reflect it back to the world in the multiplicity of color, fire and warmth thus displaying its true nature!

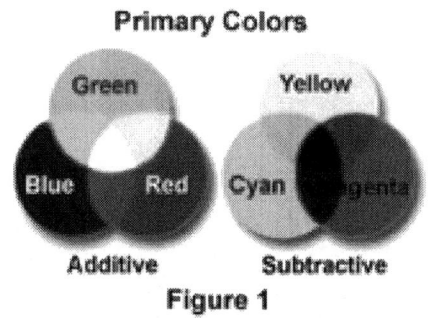

Primary Colors

Figure 1

This is exactly what the Church was originally created and designed for. The Church is not a burial society, a welfare line, a friendship club or a place to go to Heaven from. The Church was designed, to show the manifold or multifaceted wisdom of God.

Ephesians 3:10-11

> *to the intent that now the manifold wisdom of God might be made known by the church to the principalities and powers in the heavenly places, 11 according to the eternal purpose which He accomplished in Christ Jesus our Lord*

The Church was created to show the brilliance and true characteristics of God. The Church is here to prove to the universe how wide the reach and understanding of God is, that His wisdom expands beyond human comprehension. For the Word says His ways are not our ways! The parallels of the brilliant diamond and the church are uncanny.

Let me show you below:

The Brilliant Diamond The Church

- Designed to receive light Designed to receive revelation of the Kingdom
- Designed with a table Designed as the entrance of revelation of the Kingdom
- Reflects on seven spectrums Reflects on the seven mountains of earthly influence

The brilliant diamond has another specific design that differentiates it from all other gemstone designs - depth. It is very important that we talk about the depth of the brilliant diamond. Depth determines how much light the diamond can capture. Diagram 2 shows how the ideal cut diamond captures the most light. In the other designs light passes through but is not captured and most importantly is not reflected. The Bible tells us in Ephesians 3:17 that as disciples of Christ we are to be both rooted and grounded in love.

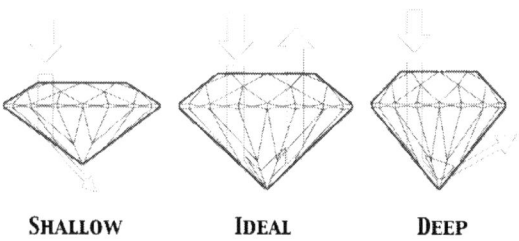

SHALLOW   **IDEAL**   **DEEP**

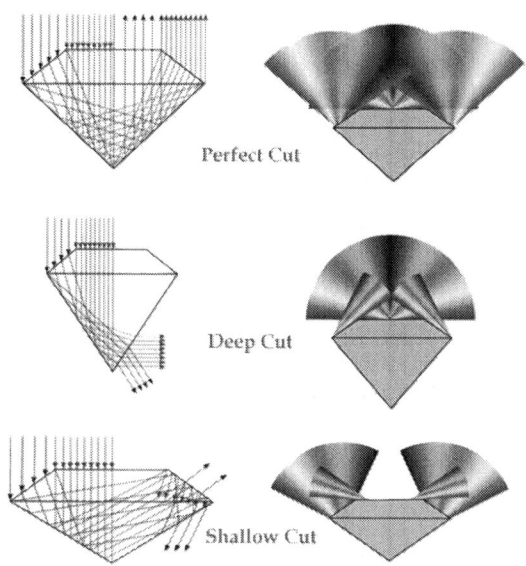

Perfect Cut

Deep Cut

Shallow Cut

Ephesian 3:17 so that Christ may dwell in your hearts through faith. And I pray that you, being rooted and established in love.

We're supposed to have Christ in our hearts and be rooted and grounded in love. If we're not rooted, we will find that we'll just wither away. Thus, we have to desire the truth and grow strong in Christ. We have to be rooted and built up in Christ through being taught the truth. This process isn't an overnight process either. The process of being rooted, grounded, and settled in Christ requires a continual work for each one of us to do.

We have to be rooted and built up in Christ through being taught the truth.

As we just read, our being rooted and grounded in Christ keeps us settled. The word translated as "settled" is from the Greek word "hedraios". Using Thayer's Dictionary and the Strong's number 1476, you find this word means: "firm, unmovable, steadfast". Rather than being tossed to and from, we're supposed to be settled, firm, unmovable, steadfast. I am telling you, we do not need any more half-hearted churches cropping up across the world. God has made it very clear on what He expects!

Allow me to speak plainly. We don't need deep churches. We don't need shallow churches. We need brilliant churches! We need churches that build on the original idea and intent of the Creator, churches purposely planted that show all of His glory. We need churches to model the very nature of our King!

We don't need deep churches. We don't need shallow churches. We need brilliant churches!

I have a question for you...what should happen when the light of the revelation of the Kingdom hits or engages with the Church? What should happen is the same effect that happens to the brilliant diamond when light hits it. The Church should sparkle and shine with the original idea of God. It is the portal and gate by which God intended to lead, manage and influence the earth's systems.

The Church was not designed as an afterthought. The Church is not here just to get people saved and then raptured out of here. It was to get people restored to the original design and send them into the world with the goal of redeeming the world back to God.

We need churches to model the very nature of our King!

Whatever God is doing in the earth, it will be done through the Church! If it's not of the Church, God is not involved with it! The Church should be on fire as it was in Acts Chapter 2. Let's read it:

Acts 2:3 And there appeared unto them cloven tongues like as of fire, and it sat upon each of them.

Fire was how the Holy Spirit was described when it fell on the saints in the Upper Room. Often when people see a brilliant cut diamond they say it is on "fire." What does fire mean when it refers to diamonds and how does it happen?

The Church should sparkle and shine with the original idea of God.

Fire in a diamond is the rainbow of colors that is reflected back to the eye from the diamond. Light enters through the top of the diamond, is broken down into a rainbow of spectral colors, and is reflected back and forth in the interior of the gem by bouncing off the mirror-like facets. When it leaves through the crown, it stays separated and reaches the eye in flashes of color. Like all types and cuts of diamonds, some just seem to shine and sparkle more than others depending on the clarity and grade. The "Church" is to be like a city on a hill.

The Church was not designed as an afterthought.

Fire happens when the revelation of the Kingdom comes through the Church then this revelation is put into context of all of the systems or kingdoms of the world, if you will. When revelation leaves the Church and enters the world, it engages the systems of the world with the wisdom of God. This is fire! It sparkles with brilliance because, finally, the kingdoms of this world are in the right hands, the original hands approved by God. Let's set the Church on fire!

One of the greatest tragedies in the American Church is what I call the tragedy of "Ho-Hum Christianity." The tragedy is a dry-eyed, half-hearted Church in a hell-bent nation. There were seven churches in Asia-Minor, what we would call Turkey today. The Lord gave a message to these seven churches then and He is giving a message to our Church today.

Whatever God is doing in the earth, it will be done through the Church!

These seven churches speak to us prophetically. They show to us collectively the past and the future. These messages also speak to us practically. In my opinion, there is not a problem in the local church that is not somewhere addressed in these seven churches. The problem remains, when are we going to wake up and face truth?

They also speak to us powerfully. This is the Word of God for us. God is asking, "Are you listening? He says, "Those who have ears let them hear." This is not a message for your neighbor but to you as pastors, apostles, and all church leaders. These seven churches speak to us personally. God is going to hold us responsible for the truth we have heard or we would have heard if we had listened. The sad truth about this all is that God's Church is going to be built with or without you!

DR. MARTIN WILLIAMS

CHAPTER
10

DR. MARTIN WILLIAMS

You and the Church

Nothing on earth will happen without me!
~Dr. Martin Williams

So what does this have to do with me you ask? When we talk about the Church often times we perceive it as an organization and not as an organism. The Church is not some hieratical management system that operates like a machine with no feeling. The Church is an organism, made of many parts that serve and function together to one end. The Church is a collection of purposed people who become a part of a body that moves together to fulfill the ultimate purpose; God's will on earth. Paul describes the church as a body with many members. Let's read;

Romans 12:3-5 For I say, through the grace given to

me, to everyone who is among you, not to think of himself more highly than he ought to think, but to think soberly, as God has dealt to each one a measure of faith. 4 For as we have many members in one body, but all the members do not have the same function, 5 so we, being many, are one body in Christ, and individually members of one another.

Paul reminds us that it is improper to think of ourselves as too important in this world because we do not and cannot stand alone. We are a part of something bigger than us individually. Sober thinking causes us to recognize God's design for our lives; that we were created to be a part of something much bigger - The Church!

As a matter of fact, each one of us was created, designed and gifted to be a part of the church. Each of us is expect to take an active role in the Church. Each one of us is called to function inside the Church. As a matter of fact, we are useless to the world if we are not connected and flowing in submission to the Church. My faith, which is my action base on what I believe, does not even work properly outside the leadership of the Church.

I am who I am, but I was designed to be a part of one body.

To this point, Paul reminds us that all of us together make one body, one church. I am who I am, but I was designed to be a part of one body. My hand is talented and gifted, but it would not work very well if it were not attached to my body. So it is with you and me. You and I don't necessarily have the same function, but we must be committed to one another and connected to the body called the Church. Paul continues by writing these words:

> *Romans 12:6-8 Having then gifts differing according to the grace that is given to us, let us use them: if prophecy, let us prophesy in proportion to our faith; 7 or ministry, let us use it in our ministering; he who teaches, in teaching; 8 he who exhorts, in exhortation; he who gives, with liberality; he who leads, with diligence; he who shows mercy, with cheerfulness.*

It seems that Paul is committed to reminding us that we were created, given particular gifts and required to appropriate them in order to bring glory to His name.

So back to you; what does all of this have to do with you? Everything. You see, without you, your talents, your gifts and your involvement in the church, it is impossible for it to become brilliant.

Here is what you should do to become engaged in the Church:

Recognize your creation and acknowledge that you were created by God for a specific purpose.

Genesis1:26-27 And God said, Let us make man in our image, after our likeness: and let them have dominion over the fish of the sea, and over the fowl of the air, and over the cattle, and over all the earth, and over every creeping thing that creepeth upon the earth. 27 So God created man in his own image, in the image of God created he him; male and female created he them.

Return to Your Creator

Understand that since Adam's sin in Genesis 3 you have been separated from God and need to be restored which is your decision.

Romans 10:9-11 that if you confess with your mouth the Lord Jesus and believe in your heart that God has raised Him from the dead, you will be saved. 10 For with the heart one believes unto righteousness, and with the mouth confession is made unto salvation. 11 For the Scripture says, "Whoever believes on Him will not be put to shame."

Become Part of a Kingdom Church

In order to fulfill your God given purpose you need to be a part of a Kingdom Church, so that you operate under biblical instruction and flow in Kingdom activities.

Hebrews 10:23-25 Let us hold fast the confession of our hope without wavering, for He who promised is faithful. 24 And let us consider one another in order to stir up love and good works, 25 not forsaking the assembling of ourselves together, as is the manner of some, but exhorting one another, and so much the more as you see the Day approaching.

Discover and Accept Your Spiritual Gift

Becoming familiar with your gifts and skills is paramount to your success and the Kingdom's success. Accepting these will cause you fit in the body and your gifts to be deployed at the highest levels.

—

Skill is developed over time.

1 Corinthians 12:4-11 There are diversities of gifts, but the same Spirit. 5 There are differences of ministries, but the same Lord. 6 And there are diversities of activities, but it is the same God who works all in all. 7 But the manifestation of the Spirit is given to each one for the profit of all: 8 for to one is given the word of wisdom through the Spirit, to another the word of knowledge through the same Spirit, 9 to another faith by the same Spirit, to another gifts of healings by the same Spirit, 10 to another the working of miracles, to another prophecy, to another discerning of spirits, to another different kinds of tongues, to another the interpretation of tongues. 11 But one and the same Spirit works all these things, distributing to each one individually as He wills.

Become Skilled at Your Spiritual Gift

Skill is developed over time in the proper environment

and under the right mentoring. You simply have to be part of and submitted to leadership to get this done.

> *Ephesians 4:11-12 And He Himself gave some to be apostles, some prophets, some evangelists, and some pastors and teachers, 12 for the equipping of the saints for the work of ministry, for the edifying of the body of Christ,*

Serve God with Your Spiritual Gifts Through the Church.

Don't wait until you are perfect before you begin to be a part of a local church and serve your gifts. Your life depends on it and so does the brilliant church.

> *1 Peter 4:10-11 As each one has received a gift, minister it to one another, as good stewards of the manifold grace of God. 11 If anyone speaks, let him speak as the oracles of God. If anyone ministers, let him do it as with the ability which God supplies, that in all things God may be glorified through Jesus Christ, to whom belong the glory and the dominion forever and ever. Amen.*

Conclusion

The cut of a diamond refers not to its shape only but to the balanced of proportion, symmetry and polish achieved by the diamond cutter. Likewise the church that you lead or attend should be balance and be specifically patterned according to God's original Church model. What makes a church brilliant is not its denomination, money, buildings or its leadership team. What makes a church brilliant is its' proportion, symmetry and polish achieved by the radiance of the King.

The extent of how well the diamond is cut is directly related to the diamond's overall beauty. I did not write this book because I lead or attend a brilliant church but because I discovered the beautiful purpose of the King's Church idea. God's purpose of, ability in and call to the Church is brilliant and beautiful. It is my hope that I can be a part of a local Church and a universal Church that restores beauty to the world.

> *What makes a church brilliant is not its denomination, money, buildings or its leadership team.*

When a diamond has been correctly cut, the diamond's ability to reflect and refract light is greatly enhanced. The prayer is that the church will return to the brilliant idea of reflecting and refracting the light or Kingdom revelation of God. The ideal Church will receive knowledge and revelation about God's Kingdom. The ideal Church will reflect that Kingdom knowledge and revelation onto the systems of this world. These revelations will bring healing and restoration anywhere that they are applied. This revelation will refract or become adaptable to any kingdom of this world it interacts with. The seven mountains of Family, Education, Government, Media, Church, Business and Health will be dramatically changed and healed when the revelation of the Kingdom shines on them.

By understanding the way that light moves through diamond crystals, modern diamond cutters have established a specific set of proportions and angles that are known to harness the diamond's internal brilliance and to show it in its best light. Respectfully, more and more leaders of churches around the world are discovering the King's original concept of Church. Many are receiving revelation and are being enlightened by the Holy Spirt on how to return the Church to the original idea of the King.

The prayer is that the church will return to the brilliant idea of reflecting and refracting the light or Kingdom revelation of God.

I myself am striving, praying and tapping into other brilliant leaders to learn more about how the church can impact the worlds with the Kingdom message restoring them back to God.

After all, the Church is the most important entity on planet earth!

Haggai 2:6-9

This is what the Lord Almighty says: 'In a little while I will once more shake the heavens and the earth, the sea and the dry land. 7 I will shake all nations, and the desire of all nations will come, and I will fill this house with glory,' says the Lord Almighty. 8 'The silver is mine and the gold is mine,' declares the Lord Almighty. 9 'The glory of this present house will be greater than the glory of the former house,' says the Lord Almighty. 'And in this place I will grant peace,' declares the Lord Almighty."

DR. MARTIN WILLIAMS

ABOUT THE AUTHOR

Martin L. Williams is a phenomenal leader and global speaker. His straight forward speaking talent is amazingly thought provoking. He is sought after and frequently travels nationally and internationally sharing life-changing principles and concepts.

He has published several books. The first, "All Marriages Are Not Created Equal" is co-authored with his wife, Lynnell. His books have been proven tools to assist men and women from all walks of life in getting their lives moving in the right direction both spiritually and naturally. The eye-opening concepts found in his writings will get you moving forward and in hot pursuit of your personal purpose.

Dr. Williams has a gift that touches the very heart of every individual he encounters, especially when sharing truths of leadership. He is a visionary leader with an insightful awareness of what people need to succeed and how he can empower them for success. This is the heart of true leadership. Although people are our most valuable asset the Church is the most important institution on planet earth.

DR. MARTIN WILLIAMS

Eight Enemies of Vision
Vision Wakes Up Opposition

In this book Dr. Martin Williams explains vision and its enemies. These enemies must be identified, confronted and overcome in order for you to fulfill your vision hence completing your life assignment. This book "Eight Enemies of Vision" was written to assist you through this process.

DR. MARTIN WILLIAMS

Equipping Leaders
Spiritual Gifts Training Manual

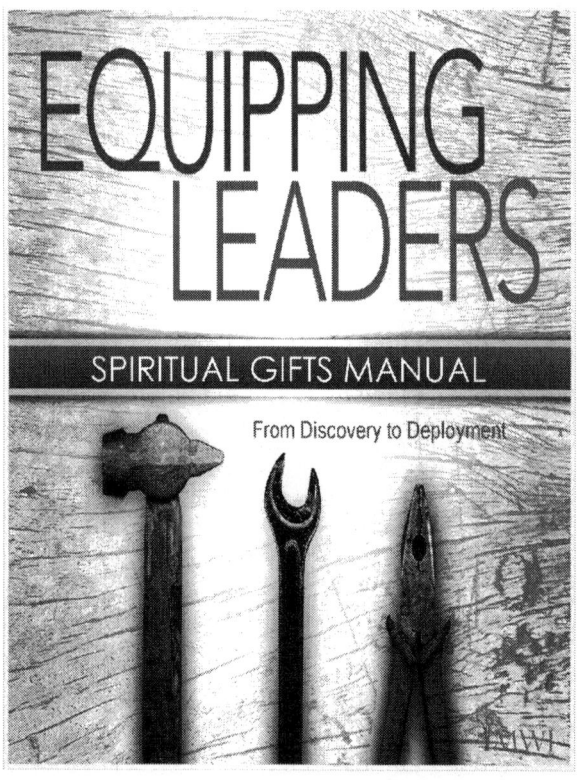

Comprehensive training of the 12 Spiritual Gifts. This teaching series has been assembled for you to take a closer look at ways you can become more involved in what the apostle Paul calls, "the work of ministry." You have been given a mandate to go into all the world and be ambassadors with the right message and tools to expand God's influence around the world.

Additional books by Dr. Martin Williams are available for purchase at www.martinwilliams.org

Raise Your Expectations
(Forwarded by Dr. Myles Munroe)

Ignorance: What You Don't Know

Can I Get A Witness?: The Kingdom Manifested on Earth

Exhale: Blow Your Own Trumpet

All Marriages Are Not Created Equal
(Written by Martin & Lynnell Williams)

15 Days to Joy
(Forwarded by Jesse Duplaints)

Why Am I Here?: Children's Book by Joshua Williams
(Forwarded by Dr. Myles Munroe)

[i] The late Dr. Myles Munroe is the visionary of Bahamas Faith Ministries International and Myles Munroe International. Dr. Munroe is also founder of the International Third World Leaders Association (ITWLA). He has written over 38 books addressing the Kingdom and critical issues affecting every aspect of human, professional, leadership, social, and spiritual development. Dr. Munroe's greatest blessing in his life is his dedicated wife, the late Ruth Munroe and their two children, Myles (Chario) and Charisa; he says that his family is his greatest responsibility and his marriage his most sacred trust.

63085830R00087

Made in the USA
Lexington, KY
26 April 2017